Human Life Cycles

Anita Ganeri

Heinemann
LIBRARY

young
Explorer

www.heinemann.co.uk/library
Visit our website to find out more information about **Heinemann Library** books.

To order:
☎ Phone 44 (0) 1865 888066
🖹 Send a fax to 44 (0) 1865 314091
🖥 Visit the Heinemann Bookshop at www.heinemann.co.uk/library to browse our catalogue and order online.

First published in Great Britain by Heinemann Library, Halley Court, Jordan Hill, Oxford OX2 8EJ, part of Harcourt Education. Heinemann is a registered trademark of Harcourt Education Ltd.

Editorial: Jilly Attwood, Kate Bellamy
Design: Jo Hinton-Malivoire
Picture research: Kay Altwegg, Ruth Blair
Production: Séverine Ribierre

Originated by Dot Gradations Ltd
Printed and bound in China by South China Printing Company

ISBN 0 431 11408 0 (hardback)
09 08 07 06 05
10 9 8 7 6 5 4 3 2 1

ISBN 0 431 11414 5 (paperback)
10 09 08 07 06
10 9 8 7 6 5 4 3 2 1

British Library Cataloguing in Publication Data
Ganeri, Anita
Human Life Cycles – (Nature's Patterns)
612.6
A full catalogue record for this book is available from the British Library.

Acknowledgements
The Publishers would like to thank the following for permission to reproduce photographs: Corbis pp. **20** (Will and Deni McIntyre), **28** (Don Mason), **7** (Tim Pannell), **21** (Peter Saloutos), **19** (Ariel Skelley); Getty pp. **11** (Clarissa Leahy), **29** (John Terence Turner); Harcourt pp. **5**, **6**, **8**, **9**, **14**, **16**, **17**, **30**; Photodisc pp. **5**, **23**, **24**, **25**, **26**, **27**, **30**; Science Photo Library pp. **15** (Mark Clarke), **18** (Laura Dwight), **10** (Edelman), **13** (Ian Hooton), **12** (Sovereign, ISM).

Cover photograph of a family group is reproduced with permission of Corbis.

Our thanks to David Lewin for his assistance in the preparation of this book.

Every effort has been made to contact copyright holders of any material reproduced in this book. omissions will be rectified in subsequent printings if notice is given to the Publishers.

The paper used to print this book comes from sustainable resources.

Contents

Words appearing in the text in bold, **like this**, are explained in the Glossary.

 Find out more about Nature's Patterns at www.heinemannexplore.co.uk

Nature's patterns

Nature is always changing. Many of the changes that happen follow a **pattern**. This means that they happen over and over again.

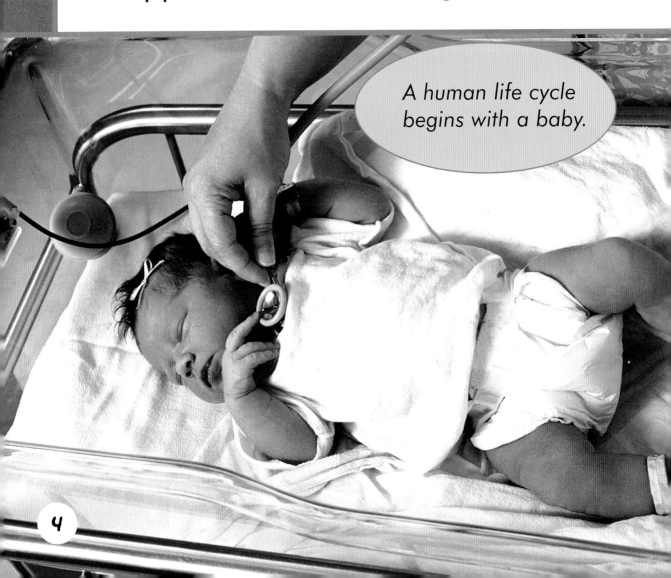

A human life cycle begins with a baby.

Older people may have grandchildren. These are the children of their children.

A human life cycle is a kind of pattern. It is how a person is born, grows up, gets old and finally dies.

Growing and changing

When a human baby is born, he or she looks like a tiny copy of their parents. The baby gets older, and grows up to be a child.

Children start off as tiny babies.

Babies grow into adults and then they can have their own babies.

A child's body carries on changing as it grows to become an **adult**. Adults can have babies of their own. Then the life cycle **pattern** starts again.

Starting life

The people in the picture below all look different. Some of them are tall and some are short. Some have blue eyes and some have brown eyes. Some have dark hair and some have light hair.

Everyone is different but all human beings have a similar life cycle. They all start life inside their mother's body.

A baby begins

A baby grows in a special place inside her mother's tummy. This place is called the womb. The baby needs food and **oxygen** to grow. She gets these from her mother.

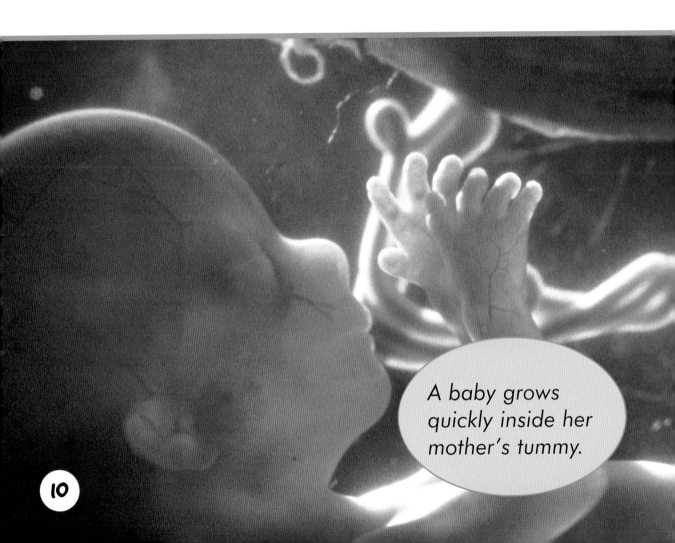

A baby grows quickly inside her mother's tummy.

Your tummy button shows where the tube used to join you to your mother.

Food and oxygen reach the baby through a tube. The tube joins the baby to her mother when she is growing inside the mother.

The baby grows

For the next nine months, the baby grows inside her mother. She soon looks like a tiny human being. She sleeps and wakes up. She even gets hiccups.

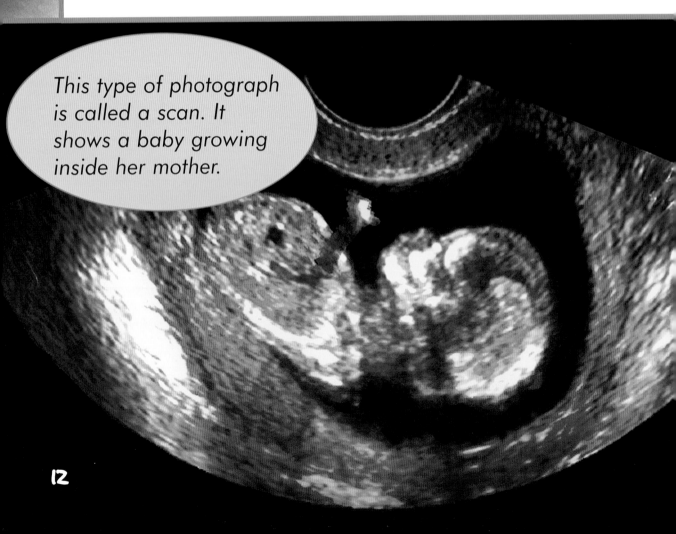

This type of photograph is called a scan. It shows a baby growing inside her mother.

As the baby grows bigger, the mother's tummy gets bigger, too. The baby moves about inside her mother. Sometimes the baby kicks the mother with her legs.

When a woman has a baby growing inside her, she is pregnant.

Being born

After nine months, the baby is ready to be born. She turns upside-down inside her mother's tummy. Then she squeezes out of her mother's body.

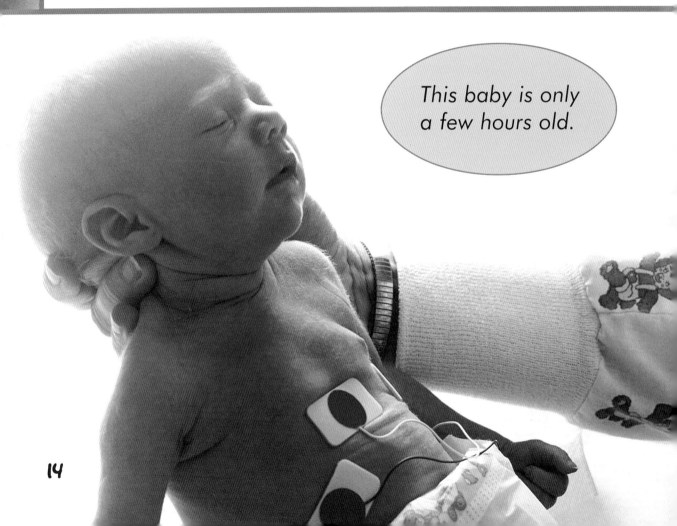

This baby is only a few hours old.

These are identical twins. That means they look exactly like each other.

Sometimes a mother gives birth to two babies at the same time. They are called twins. Some twins look exactly like each other. Some twins look different from each other.

Feeding and learning

At first, the baby drinks her mother's milk. This helps her to grow up strong and healthy. Later, she starts to eat solid food.

Milk has lots of **nutrients** to help the baby grow.

Babies learn how to hold, grip and pull things by playing with toys.

The baby learns about the world. She learns to smile, laugh and make sounds. She also learns to sit up on her own and to crawl about.

Growing Up

When the baby is about 18 months old, she is called a **toddler**. Her muscles grow stronger and she can walk on her own. She also starts to speak in proper words.

As children grow, they learn how to see shapes and colours, and the world around them.

A child grows quickly again at the age of ten.

In the first two years, a toddler grows very fast. Her bones get longer and make her taller. Humans carry on growing until they are about 18 to 20 years old.

Teenagers

From the age of 13, a child is called a **teenager**. Around this age a child starts to grow into an **adult**. Changes happen in a teenager's body so one day they will be able to have children.

It is important for teenagers to eat healthy food because their bodies are growing and changing.

It is important for children to eat a **balanced diet** when they are growing up. Taking exercise, like swimming or playing a sport, will help them to stay healthy.

Adult life

When a **teenager** is about 18 years old, he or she is an **adult**. Their bodies stop changing so quickly.

Adults' bodies have stopped growing but they still need to stay healthy and exercise.

This mother has a new baby. The baby will grow up to become an adult like her.

Many adults have babies. The life cycle **pattern** starts again. Their babies grow into **toddlers**, then teenagers. Then they become adults.

23

Middle age

People are middle aged when they reach about 50 years old. Their bodies are changing again. Some of these changes happen inside their bodies.

When women reach middle age their bodies change so they are no longer able to have babies.

Some men begin to lose their hair and go **bald**.

Some changes caused by middle age happen on the outside of the body. When they reach middle age, some people start to look older. Their skin becomes more **wrinkled**.

Getting old

At around the ages of 60 to 70 years, people show more signs of getting older. Their skin gets more **wrinkles**. Their hair may turn grey or white.

A person's body changes a lot as they get older.

Some changes mean that old people need help to walk and move.

Older people cannot see or hear as well as when they were younger. Some people may **stoop** when they stand up. They may also find it harder to move about quickly.

The end of life

Many people live to be over 70 years old. Older people are more likely to become ill. Eating a **balanced diet** and taking exercise helps them to stay healthy.

Many older people still live active lives.

It can be very sad when someone dies but this is part of the life cycle **pattern**. Other children are born and grow up. Then the life cycle begins all over again.

Grandparents can be a lot of fun!

Human life cycle chart

Here you can follow the different steps in a human's life cycle. You can see how a person's body grows and changes as they get older.

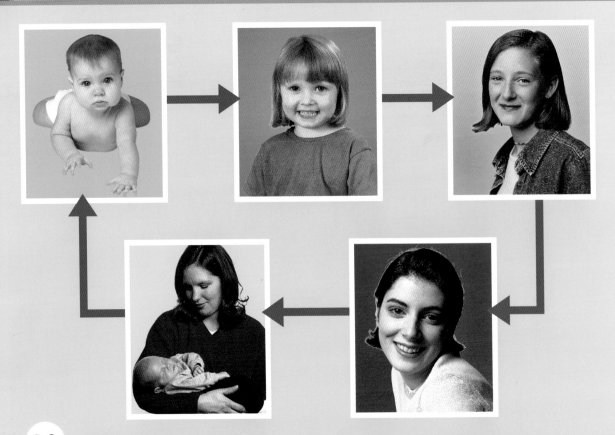

Find out more about Nature's Patterns at www.heinemannexplore.co.uk

Glossary

adult a person aged over 18, who is fully grown and can have children

balanced diet eating a good mixture of food to help you stay healthy

bald having no hair on your head

nutrients food that is needed for living things to grow

oxygen a gas in the air. People and animals need to breathe in oxygen to stay alive.

pattern something that happens over and over again

stoop to bend over slightly when you stand or walk

teenager child of about 13 to 18 years old

toddler child of about 18 months to 4 years old

wrinkle mark or line on the skin caused by age

More books to read

Growing Up, Henry Pluckrose (Franklin Watts, 2003)

Living Things: Life Cycles, Anita Ganeri (Heinemann Library, 2001)

Our World: Living and Growing, Neil Morris (Chrysalis Press, 2002)

My World of Science: Human Growth, Angela Royston (Heinemann Library, 2003)

Index